Recov

Stacey Faulkner

BookLeaf
Publishing

Presentation by *BookLeaf Publishing*

Web: www.bookleafpub.com

E-mail: info@bookleafpub.com

ISBN: 9789357696579

First edition 2023

DEDICATION

For Mum.

ACKNOWLEDGEMENT

Thank you to Mum, Suzanne, and Lesley-Anne who read these poems as I chose and wrote them over the last twenty-one days. You listened to and read so many variations of the same lines and I really value your input, thank you for caring about the thing I love most. Thank you to Lesley, I wrote one of my favourite poems outside your house while waiting to see you. Thank you to Nathan for making me laugh and Robyn for keeping me company.

- November 2022

Adulthood

You hurt the girl I used to be
and I never thought that I'd be free.

Now inside this grown up frame,
she doesn't answer when you call her name.

F Words

Fight or flight

but also freeze
and fold
and fake
and fawn
and fear.

And later,
fix.

And later,
much later,
flourish.

Recovered

I healed.

I glued and taped the broken parts
until the trauma was imperceptible.

Sometimes a loose piece
finds its way to the surface
and grazes me with a fresh shock.

Even if it cuts me, it won't be fatal now.

Haunted

The trauma visits like a ghost
long after the exorcism,
when it does you have to remember:
your body isn't the same haunted house
it once made home.

Spring

I couldn't sleep.

Frogs called out from the pond
loud with loneliness,
moaning for a lover
groaning for a friend.

Large white moths
ignored the moon,
thumping into the window
bumping desperately at the artificial light.

The night was awake with longing.

Gold

I collected small good things
with a magpie's eye for joy,
I stored them away like treasures
until they numbered higher than I could count.

I showed you my hoard,
I thought you'd shade your eyes against the glare,
but you pushed it all aside
and said there was nothing golden there.

Evergreen

I watched the seasons shift,
deciduous became a familiar word
and they tell you 'nothing blooms forever'.

I became too attentive
I over watered
and flooded the ground.

When the blackspot started
I cut the branches
to save the rest of the plant.

I learned not to mourn the leaves
when they turned and fell,
I planted new annuals and saved the seeds.

Then unchanged by the months,
standing witness over all the cycles
never succumbing to the fall,
you stood evergreen.

Unmatched

There's plenty of fish in the sea
but I don't have any bait.

Every pot has a lid
but maybe I'm a vase.

Broody

When I see a baby my ovaries hum,
the sound is audible,
like a stomach late to lunch,
I wonder if anyone can hear the difference.

There are little half-people waiting inside me,
they swell with hope
then drop away into nothing.

All that potential
going ... going ... gone.

Songs

We're all made of stardust,
that wasn't new to me,
I'd heard how all our elements
had passed through the sky
and God gathered up particles
that existed for a billion years
to build your bones out of miracles.

But I didn't think much about space
until your tiny body taught me how to hold a person
with the reverence life deserved.

Later, I learnt of quantum entanglement,
that you weren't made of crumbled stars -
you continued to be one.
I thought of us as separate from the universe
until I found out there is a star, somewhere,
still bound to you,
moving with your voice,
affected by your call.

The stars were recorded singing,
but only because they knew you first.

Prayer

So many people turn inwards
when life starts to get hard,
they put up the walls and the barricades
and struggle alone in the dark.

I always turn outwards
and reach up for You,
You give me Your light,
and I borrow Your peace,
and despite all the lions
I'm able to rest in You.

I don't talk about this
nearly as much as I should
because I know others don't believe
and they might say it's a myth.

But I know that it's true.

Unquenched

You know I love you
but you don't want it,
you like knowing it's there –
a well you can drink from
without obligation,
I give and give
and don't run dry
but I don't satisfy your thirst either.

Understudy

I spent a long time in the wings,
waiting for someone else to exit
and make space for me.
I learned the words to all the parts
so I could walk in anyone's shoes,
I'd do anything to share the stage with you.
You kept me waiting so long
I forgot I had lines of my own.

Diagnosis

See this heart all black and blue
now try to guess what it's been through,
study the x-ray's shattered break,
note each time in the night I wake.
Call a doctor, ask for advice,
read all the textbooks, check them twice,
sit down and ask me how I feel,
second-guess the best way to heal.
Ignore the fact this pain is you,
this was caused by the things you do,
you were the one to see it break,
and only you can heal this ache,
but it's much easier to pretend,
that on its own this pain will mend.

"Just"

Maybe we'll be friends
and maybe we'll find
that's a lot of love to share.

Love Triangle

It's win/win
either way I'm with someone
who excites me.

It's lose/lose
either way I've lost someone
who delights me.

Mirage

When you appeared
I didn't believe it
because before then
I'd made you up,
and how could you be any more
than a mirage of my lonely heart?

Glasses

I take off my glasses and the world blurs,
I get headaches from the haze,
but you remain clear,
and I can still make out
the constellations of your freckles
like my eyes have a memory,
the same thing that keeps me from
bumping your nose when we kiss,
without my glasses the world melts away
but then there's you ...

Sapiosexual

Without using your hands
you turn me into an ecdysiast
by gliding your tongue over
sesquipedalian delights.
You whisper the workings of the world
until I can hear the ringing of the stars
and the rhythm of the solar system
pulses through me.
Then, when I'm high and giddy on intellect,
you reduce me to a murmur of mytacism
bringing me back to Earth.
To you.

True

I worried I wouldn't find true love
because everyone warned it was so rare.

Then I realised true love, is any love,
handled with care.

Patterns

I know you with
the clarity
of souls
made from
the same substance.

No one understands
what elements
make up something
as intangible
as our souls.
Yet.

In the future,
when they can
look at them under
microscopes,
the fragments of our
biopsied souls
will crackle across
narrow glass slides
in identical patterns.

9 789357 696579